Oliver Twist

Charles Dickens

Abridged and adapted by Janice Greene

Illustrated by Shelley Matheis

A PACEMAKER CLASSIC

GLOBE FEARON
EDUCATIONAL PUBLISHER
PARAMUS, NEW JERSEY

Paramount Publishing

Supervising Editor: Stephen Feinstein
Project Editor: Karen Bernhaut
Editorial Assistant: Stacie Dozier
Art Director: Nancy Sharkey
Assistant Art Director: Armando Baéz
Production Manager: Penny Gibson
Production Editor: Nicole Cypher
Desktop Specialist: Eric Dawson
Manufacturing Supervisor: Della Smith
Marketing Manager: Marge Curson
Cover Illustration: Shelley Matheis

Printed in the United States of America
1 2 3 4 5 6 7 8 9 10 99 98 97 96 95 94

ISBN 0–835–91078–4

GLOBE FEARON
EDUCATIONAL PUBLISHER
PARAMUS, NEW JERSEY

Paramount Publishing

Contents

Cast of Characters

Oliver Twist	An orphan boy and main character in the story
Fagin	The master thief who takes in young boys as his apprentices
Nancy	A member of Fagin's gang who feels sympathy for Oliver
Bill Sikes	An associate of Fagin who tries to make Oliver into a thief
Jack Dawkins	"The artful Dodger"; a member of Fagin's gang who befriends Oliver
Mr. Bumble	The parish beadle
Mrs. Bumble	A matron of the workhouse where Oliver was born
Monks (Edward Leeford)	The evil half brother of Oliver
Mr. Brownlow	A kind gentleman who cares for Oliver
Mrs. Bedwin	Mr. Brownlow's housekeeper who never loses faith in Oliver
Mrs. Maylie	A gentlewoman who takes Oliver into her home
Rose Maylie	A young girl who has been raised as Mrs. Maylie's niece
Harry Maylie	Mrs. Maylie's son who is in love with Rose
Agnes Fleming	Oliver's mother; she dies after Oliver's birth.
Old Sally	A workhouse inmate who attends Agnes Fleming at Oliver's birth
Mr. Sowerberry	The undertaken who takes Oliver from the workhouse
Mrs. Sowerberry	The wife of Mr. Sowerberry
Charlotte	The Sowerberry's maid
Noah Claypole	A charity-boy who works for Mr. Sowerberry and later joins Fagin's gang

1 The Orphan Boy

In a certain town, which I shall not name, there is a workhouse, where the poor of the town must live. And in this workhouse, on a day and time that are not important, was born Oliver Twist.

He was brought into the world by the parish doctor and an old poor woman named Sally. At first it did not seem certain that the child would live. But then Oliver breathed, sneezed, and let out a loud cry.

At this, a young woman's head rose weakly from the pillow. "Let me see the child, and die," she said.

The young doctor said, "Oh, you must not talk about dying yet."

And Sally, quickly hiding in her pocket the bottle she had been drinking from, said, "Bless her heart, no!"

The doctor placed the child in his mother's arms. She put her cold, white lips to his forehead, looked around wildly, fell back—and died.

Sally and the doctor rubbed her hands and chest. But it was no use.

"It's over," said the doctor. "She was a good-looking girl, too. Where did she come from?"

Sally said, "She was brought here last night after they found her lying in the street. You could see she'd been walking a long way. Her shoes were torn to pieces. Where she came from, nobody knows."

The doctor lifted the woman's left hand. "Ah! The old story, I see. No wedding ring. Well, good night."

Old Sally dressed the baby boy. What a wonderful example of dress young Oliver was! Before, wrapped in a blanket, he might have been the child of a rich man. But now, dressed in old, worn-out baby clothes, he fell into his place at once. He was a workhouse child, to be kicked along through the world, looked down on by all, and pitied by none.

Oliver cried loudly. If he had known he was an orphan, left in the loving hands of those who care for the poor, he might have cried even louder.

The child was sent to a baby farm, run by a Mrs. Mann. A wise woman, indeed, was Mrs. Mann. She knew what was good for children, and what was good for herself. She kept most of the food money for herself, and did not waste much on the children.

As you can see, this kind of farming would not bring forth much of a crop. Oliver's ninth birthday found him a pale, thin child. Unlike many of the children who had come to the baby farm, however, he was still living.

It was on this day that the baby farm had a most important visitor. It was Mr. Bumble, the parish beadle. Mr. Bumble was a fat man, and most important looking with his cane and hat.

"Oliver is too old to stay here any longer," Mr. Bumble told Mrs. Mann. "He must go to the workhouse now. I myself will take him there. Bring him to me at once."

So Oliver was brought to Mr. Bumble, and the beadle led him away from the baby farm. In all the years he had spent there, Oliver had never heard a kind word. And yet he cried when he left, for it was all he had ever known.

The workhouse was a fine home for poor people. It gave them a wonderful choice. They could choose not to live there and starve quickly. Or they could live there and starve slowly. People in the workhouse were given a bowl of gruel—watered-down oatmeal—three times a day, with an onion twice a week, and half a roll on Sundays.

Oliver and the other boys grew wild with hunger. One boy, who was tall for his age, began saying he might eat one of the others if he didn't get more gruel to eat. The boys talked quietly among themselves and decided one of them must ask for more. They played a game of chance to see who must ask. It was Oliver who lost.

That evening he went up to the master, bowl in hand, and said, "Please, sir, I want some more."

The master turned pale. He stared at Oliver, his mouth open. Then he grabbed Oliver and yelled for the beadle.

The members of the workhouse board were having a meeting when Mr. Bumble burst in. "I beg your pardon, sirs!" he said. "Oliver Twist has asked for more!"

"For *more*!" cried one of the board.

Another man shook his head. "That boy will be hanged some day," he said. "I know it."

Oliver was shut up in a dark room. The next day, a notice went up in front of the workhouse. It offered five pounds to anyone who would take Oliver Twist off the hands of the workhouse.

A few days later, a man named Mr. Gamfield was walking past the workhouse with his donkey. Mr. Gamfield was a chimney sweep and was not known for his kindness. He read the notice and decided a workhouse boy might be

most useful to him. He knew what workhouse boys were fed, and felt they would be small enough to fit in a chimney.

Mr. Gamfield and Mr. Bumble struck a bargain. Mr. Bumble told Oliver the good news, which made the boy cry.

"Come, come Oliver," said Mr. Bumble. "Wipe your eyes and don't cry into your gruel. That's a very foolish thing to do." Indeed it was, for there was quite enough water in it already.

Mr. Bumble took Oliver in front of the magistrates. There were papers to be signed. One of the old magistrates lifted his pen to sign Oliver away to Mr. Gamfield. He looked for the inkwell. It was not where it should be. Then, by chance, he looked at Oliver. The boy was looking at Mr. Gamfield's cruel face with horror.

"My boy!" said the old magistrate. "You look pale and afraid. What is the matter?"

Oliver fell on his knees and begged them to do anything to him—rather than send him away with Mr. Gamfield.

"Well!" said Mr. Bumble. "Of all the little rascals!"

"Hold your tongue, beadle," said the magistrate.

Mr. Bumble could not believe what he had heard. A beadle asked to hold his tongue!

"We will not sign these papers," said the magistrate. "Take the boy back to the workhouse and treat him kindly. He seems to need it."

In the end, Oliver was given to Mr. Sowerberry, an undertaker. This time, Oliver said nothing. Mr. Bumble thought Oliver must have little feeling. But, in truth, instead of having too little feeling, Oliver had too much.

Mr. Sowerberry was a tall, thin man, who dressed all in black. He took Oliver home to Mrs. Sowerberry. She called the maid, Charlotte, and had her give the boy some meat the dog hadn't eaten. Then Oliver had a restful sleep among the coffins.

The next day, Oliver met Noah Claypole, who also worked for Mr. Sowerberry. Noah was a charity-boy, a poor boy sent to a charity school and dressed in a charity uniform. He was used to being called "charity," and looked down upon by other boys. But now Noah had the luck to find Oliver—an orphan—whom even he could look down upon. This shows us what a beautiful thing human nature is. The same fine qualities can be found in a great lord and a dirty charity-boy.

When Oliver had been at Mr. Sowerberry's for a few weeks, the undertaker asked his wife in a timid voice, "I want to ask what you think, my dear. Young Twist is a very good-looking boy. And there is a look of sadness about him that is most interesting. I do think he could come along to children's funerals. It might look nice, don't you think, dear?"

Mrs. Sowerberry did think it was a fine idea, but she was not about to tell her husband. Instead she asked him why he didn't think of it before.

Oliver went out to a funeral with Mr. Sowerberry the next day. He didn't like it, but Mr. Sowerberry told him he would get used to it in time.

Noah Claypole, of course, did not like to see Oliver in this new position, and so treated him as badly as possible in the months that followed. Charlotte treated him badly because Noah did. And Mrs. Sowerberry was his enemy because Mr. Sowerberry was friendly to him.

One evening, Noah and Oliver were waiting for dinner. Noah, hungry and feeling mean, decided to pass the time by tormenting Oliver.

"How's your mother, Workhouse?" Noah began.

"She's dead!" said Oliver. "Don't you say anything more about her to me!"

"You know, Workhouse," said Noah, "I'm very sorry for you. But you must know, your mother was a real bad one."

"What did you say?" said Oliver, looking up very quickly.

"A real bad one," said Noah. "And it's better she died when she did. Or she would have ended up in prison, or transported, or hanged."

Oliver turned red with fury. He jumped up, knocking over his chair. He grabbed Noah and shook him until the boy's teeth chattered in his head. Then, with all his strength, he knocked him to the floor.

A minute ago, Oliver had been the sad, quiet boy that cruel treatment had made him. But now his eyes were bright. He stood up tall.

"He'll murder me!" cried Noah. "Help! Charlotte! Oliver's gone mad!"

Charlotte rushed in, grabbed Oliver, and beat him with her fists. "Oh, you awful little murderer!" she cried.

Mrs. Sowerberry helped by scratching Oliver's face and Noah, seeing all was safe, got up and hit him from behind.

When Mr. Sowerberry came home, he heard of Oliver's terrible attack from his wife. It was clear that if he did not give the boy a good beating, he would be a cruel husband. He would be less than a man. So he gave Oliver a good beating indeed.

Oliver took it all without a tear. He would not cry in front of them. But that night, when he was alone, the tears came—for a very long time.

He tied up his few bits of clothes in a handkerchief and waited for the light of day. When it came, he walked quietly out of the house and started out on the road to London.

2 A Merry Old Gentleman

It was 70 miles to London, and Oliver had but a penny that Mr. Sowerberry had given him. The trip was hard and very long. But one kind man gave him a meal of bread and cheese, and a kind old lady gave him all she could. If it had not been for these two, Oliver might have ended his journey the way his mother had ended hers.

The seventh day found Oliver in the town of Barnet, just outside London. He sat by the side of the street, covered with dust. His feet were bleeding and his body was too tired to move.

After a while, he noticed that a boy was looking at him from the other side of the street. This was the strangest boy Oliver had ever seen. He was short, with sharp, ugly eyes. His hat sat so lightly on his head it seemed it would fall off any minute. He wore a man's coat that came almost to his knees.

The boy crossed the street and came up to him. "Hello! What's the row?"

"I'm tired and hungry," said Oliver. "I've been walking for seven days."

"You want grub?" said the young gentleman. "You shall have it. I'm at a low-water-mark myself. I'll fork out this time. Come on!"

He took Oliver to a shop, where he bought bread and ham. Then he took Oliver to the back of a public house, where he bought a pot of beer.

"Going to London?" asked the strange young man as they ate.

"Yes," said Oliver.

"Got any place to stay?" said the boy.

"No," said Oliver.

"Well, don't fret your eyelids on that score," said the young man, as he finished the beer. "I know a merry old gentleman that lives there. He'll give you a bed for nothing—that is, if I introduce you."

The offer of a place to sleep was too good to pass up. The strange boy went on to say that his name was Jack Dawkins, but he was called "the artful Dodger." Oliver was beginning to think his new friend was not quite respectable. But he was looking forward to meeting the merry old gentleman.

The boys reached London. The Dodger went quickly down one street and then another. Oliver hurried behind. He had never seen a dirtier place. The air was full of bad smells.

Oliver was thinking about running away when the Dodger grabbed his arm, opened a door, and pulled him inside. Then the Dodger whistled a signal and led Oliver up the dark and broken stairs to a room at the back of the building.

The ceiling was black with age and dirt. There was a fire, and a large table in front of it. On the table burned a candle, which was stuck into a beer bottle. Standing over the fire, frying some sausages, was a shriveled old man. His evil-looking face was almost hidden by a mass of dirty red hair. There were several beds made of old sacks around the floor. Sitting around the table were several boys, smoking and drinking as if they were middle-aged men.

"This is him, Fagin," said the Dodger. "My friend Oliver Twist."

The old man grinned and bowed. The boys gathered around Oliver, very kindly taking away his cap and the clothes he was carrying, and emptying his pockets.

They all ate supper. After that, Oliver was given something to drink, and he slept until late the next morning.

When he woke, he lay in bed, his eyes almost shut. He was not asleep, but not really awake, either. No one was in the room but Fagin.

After making coffee, Fagin looked closely at Oliver. When the boy made no move or sound, Fagin pulled up a board from the floor. He took out a box and opened it, his eyes shining. From the box he slowly lifted a sparkling gold watch— then rings, bracelets, and all sorts of other fine jewels.

Suddenly Fagin happened to look at Oliver. The boy was staring at him, his eyes wide open. Fagin closed the box lid with a crash and grabbed a bread knife from the table.

"What do you watch me for?" he cried. "Why are you awake? Speak out, boy! Quick! For your life!"

"I couldn't sleep any longer, sir," said Oliver. "I'm sorry if I bothered you, sir."

"Were you awake an hour ago?" said Fagin.

"On my word, I was not, sir," said Oliver.

"Tush, tush, my dear," said Fagin, putting the knife down. "Of course, you were not. I was only trying to scare you. You're a brave boy. Ha! Ha! . . . er, did you see any of these pretty things in the box?"

"Yes, sir," said Oliver.

"Ah!" said Fagin, turning a little pale. "They're mine, Oliver. All I have to live on in my old age. People call me a miser, my dear."

Oliver thought the old man must truly be a miser, to live in such a dirty place, with so many watches. When Oliver got up to wash his face, the box had disappeared.

He had just finished cleaning up when the Dodger came back, along with one of the other boys, Charley Bates. The four sat down to eat breakfast.

After the meal was cleared away, Charley Bates and the Dodger played a strange game with Fagin. Fagin would walk about the room. The two boys would follow him for a while, then they would accidentally bump into him. Next, they would very quickly take from him his handkerchief, shirt-pin, snuff box, watch, watch chain, and even his glasses case.

While the three were all playing this game, a young lady came to see Fagin. Her name was Nancy. She had a lot of hair, not fixed very neatly. She was not pretty exactly, but she had a lively way about her and a great deal of color in her face. Oliver thought her a very nice girl. After a long visit, where everyone had something to drink, Nancy, Charley Bates, and the Dodger went off to work.

Oliver had no idea what this work was, but he wanted very much to join in. At last, after many days, Fagin let him go out with the Dodger and Charley Bates.

The three boys walked along the busy streets. To Oliver, it did not seem they were going anywhere. Then, the Dodger suddenly put a finger to his lips.

"See that old man over there, looking at books?" said the Dodger. He pointed to a respectable-looking old gentleman with a powdered head and gold glasses. He had taken a book from a bookseller's stall and was very busy reading.

"He'll do," said Charley Bates.

As Oliver watched, the Dodger walked quietly up to the old man, reached in his pocket, and drew out his handkerchief! He handed the handkerchief to Charley Bates, and the two of them ran off around the corner, full speed.

All at once, Oliver knew the reason for the strange game Fagin played with the boys. He stood there, his blood burning, filled with horror. Then, confused and frightened, he began to run.

That same moment, the old man noticed his handkerchief was gone. He saw Oliver running away and shouted, "Stop thief!"

As soon as they saw him running, the Dodger and Charley Bates also shouted, "Stop thief!" and began to run after Oliver. People stopped what they were doing and took up the chase. In a few minutes, the terrified boy was caught. A police officer dragged him to the police station. Some of the crowd followed, and with them was the old gentleman whose handkerchief was stolen.

After a long wait in a dirty cell and many questions, Oliver was very pale and weak.

The old gentleman, whose name was Mr. Brownlow, was worried. "I'm really not sure the boy took the handkerchief," he said. "And he seems to be quite ill."

"Nonsense," said the officer. "I know better."

Oliver was about to be sentenced to hard labor, when the bookseller hurried in.

"I saw it all," said the man. "I'm the one who was selling the gentleman the books. The robbery was done by another boy!"

"All right then, let the boy go!" said the officer in an angry voice.

Mr. Brownlow left the police station and walked out into the yard. There he saw little Oliver, who had been set free a few minutes earlier. The boy lay on his back on the side of the street, his face a deadly white.

"Poor, poor boy!" said Mr. Brownlow, bending over him. "Call a coach, somebody. Hurry!"

3 Saved and Lost Again

The coach started away, with Oliver and Mr. Brownlow in it, to another part of London. It went down a quiet, shady street and stopped before a neatly kept house. Oliver was gently carried inside and put to bed.

In the days that followed, the boy was cared for with more kindness than he had ever known. But he was unaware of it, for the fever held him and he knew not where he was.

At last he woke. He said weakly, "What room is this?"

Mrs. Bedwin, the housekeeper, hurried to his side. She was an old woman, very neatly dressed. "Hush, my dear," she said. "You must be very quiet, so you can get well." She gently smoothed the hair from his forehead, and the boy fell asleep again.

Soon the fever was gone, and Oliver was able to eat a little. Mrs. Bedwin brought him some strong broth. Oliver looked at the broth and thought it would be enough to feed 300 boys at the workhouse, after water was added to it.

While Oliver was eating, there was a soft knock at the door, and Mr. Brownlow came in.

When he saw the boy looking much better, the tears started in his eyes. In truth, Mr. Brownlow's heart was large enough for six old gentlemen.

Suddenly, Mr. Brownlow looked startled. "Good gracious, what's this?" he cried. "Mrs. Bedwin, look, look here!" He pointed to the picture of a young woman above Oliver's head, then at Oliver's face. The boy's face was a living copy. The eyes, the head, the mouth— everything was the same.

When Oliver had been caught, Charley Bates and the Dodger ran quickly out of sight. In a little while they were back at Fagin's.

When he saw the boys had returned without Oliver, the old man was furious.

"What's become of the boy?" cried Fagin. He grabbed the Dodger's coat collar and shook him hard.

The Dodger said, "The traps have got him. Let go o' me, will you!" He swung out of his coat, leaving Fagin holding it. Then he grabbed a long fork and made a pass at Fagin's stomach.

Fagin jumped back very quickly for an old man and threw a pot at him.

"What the blazes is going on now?" said a deep voice. A man of about 35 stepped into the room. He was a big man, with very dirty pants

about his thick legs and a dirty handkerchief around a strong neck. A white dog, its face scratched and torn in 20 places, followed him into the room.

"Why, good morning, Bill Sikes, my dear," said Fagin. "We were just talking about our young friend, Oliver Twist, who has had an unlucky time this morning." And he told Bill Sikes what had happened. "I'm afraid," added Fagin, "that he may say something that will get us into trouble."

"That's very likely," said Sikes with a nasty grin. "You're blowed upon, Fagin."

"If that happened, I'm afraid it might come out rather the worse for you than for me, my dear."

Sikes looked angrily at Fagin. "Someone must find out what's been going on," he said.

Fagin agreed. But, as it happened, none of the boys nor Bill Sikes truly wanted to visit the police station. Just then Nancy arrived.

"The very thing!" said Fagin, and he explained to Nancy what needed to be done.

"She'll go," said Sikes.

"No, *she* won't!" said Nancy.

But after many bribes, promises, and threats, she agreed to go to the station. Fagin decided he must move quickly. He told Nancy, Charley Bates, and the Dodger, "We must know where

Oliver is. Do nothing but search until he is found! We must shut up shop tonight. Go now! And don't come to me until you have news of him."

Meanwhile, Oliver was growing stronger every day, and happy days they were. One day, Mrs. Bedwin said he was well enough to get dressed and go downstairs to visit with Mr. Brownlow. She dressed him in a new suit of clothes and gave his old clothes to one of the servants to sell.

Mr. Brownlow had Oliver come into his study. Now that the boy was well, Mr. Brownlow wanted to hear where he had come from. He also wanted to know who had raised Oliver and how he had happened to be with thieves. "Let me hear your story," said Mr. Brownlow. "Tell the truth, and you shall never be without a friend."

Oliver cried for some minutes, then began to tell how he had been brought up on the baby farm. But as he was speaking, there was an impatient knock on the door downstairs.

It was Mr. Brownlow's friend, Mr. Grimwig. He was a rather fat old gentleman, who walked with a cane. He had a way of twisting his head to one side when he spoke, which made him look a little like a parrot.

Once Oliver had met Mr. Grimwig, Mr. Brownlow sent the boy downstairs to ask Mrs. Bedwin about the tea.

"He's a nice-looking boy, is he not?" asked Mr. Brownlow.

Mr. Grimwig had thought that Oliver *was* a nice-looking boy, but he liked nothing better than to oppose his friend. He said Mrs. Bedwin had better count the silverware at night, to make sure Oliver hadn't taken any of it.

Mr. Brownlow just smiled. He was used to his friend.

As fate would have it, Mrs. Bedwin came in with some books that a boy had just delivered. They came from the same bookseller that had helped free Oliver.

"Tell the boy to wait," said Mr. Brownlow. "I have some books I want to send back with him."

"I'm sorry, sir," said Mrs. Bedwin, "But he's already gone."

"Well, then send Oliver with the books," said Mr. Grimwig.

"Oh, do let me take them, if you please, sir," said Oliver. "I'll run all the way."

Mr. Brownlow looked at his friend, who was smiling an ironic smile.

"You *shall* go, Oliver," said Mr. Brownlow. "The books are on a chair by my table. Fetch them down." He gave Oliver five pounds, for the money he owed, and directions to the bookseller's stall. Oliver set off in a hurry.

Mr. Brownlow took out his watch. "He'll be back in 20 minutes," he said, smiling at Mr. Grimwig.

After a long time it grew dark. The old gentlemen still sat in silence, the watch between them.

Oliver was walking quickly toward the bookseller's when a young woman's voice called out, "Oh, my dear brother!" He was stopped by a pair of arms thrown tightly around his neck.

"Don't!" cried Oliver. "Who is it? Let me go!"

"Oh, I've found you at last!" cried Nancy, for it was she. "You must come home, you bad boy!"

Oliver looked at her, his mouth open. "Why, it's Nancy!" he said.

"You see how he knows me," said Nancy, to the people around her. "He must come home, or he'll break his mother's—and father's—heart!"

Bill Sikes came up to them. "Come home to your mother, Oliver!" he said.

"Help!" cried Oliver. "I don't belong to them. Help! Help!" He tried to run, but Bill Sikes held him hard.

"I'll help you, you young rascal!" said Bill Sikes. "What books are these? You've been stealing, have you?" He grabbed the books from Oliver and hit him on the head.

"That's right," said a man looking out his window. "That's the only way."

"It'll do him good!" said a woman.

Bill Sikes hit Oliver again, and grabbed him by the collar. "Come along, Oliver! Here, Bull's-eye," he said to his dog. "Mind him, mind him!"

The dog growled up at Oliver. What could the poor child do but let himself be taken away?

4 The Robbery

"We're very, very happy to see you again, Oliver, my dear," said Fagin. "Why didn't you write, and say you were coming? We would have gotten something warm for supper!"

Charley Bates laughed long and loud at this, and the Dodger went through Oliver's pockets. After a short argument between Fagin and Bill Sikes, the five-pound note Oliver had ended up with Sikes.

While the two men were talking, Oliver suddenly jumped up and ran from the room, calling loudly for help. The Dodger and Charley Bates started up after him.

"Don't call Bull's-eye on him, Bill!" begged Nancy. She jumped up and closed the door, then grabbed Bill's arm. "Keep your dog back, or he'll tear the boy to pieces!"

"Serve him right," said Bill. "Stand off me, or I'll split your skull against the wall!"

"The boy won't be torn down by the dog!" screamed Nancy. "Not unless you kill me first!"

Sikes threw Nancy away from him, just as the boys came back, holding Oliver between them.

"So you wanted to get away, my dear, did you?" said Fagin, catching Oliver by the arm. "Wanted to call the police? We'll soon cure you of that." He picked up a club which lay on the corner of the fireplace.

Oliver watched him, breathing quickly. Fagin gave Oliver a smart blow on the shoulders. Nancy rushed up and pulled the club from his hands. She threw it in the fire.

She screamed, "Let the boy be! Or I'll put such a mark on you that will bring me to the gallows! You've got the boy, now. He'll soon be a liar and a thief, just like me!"

Fagin backed away from her, for she was frightening to see. "Well, well," he said, trying to calm her, "after all, it's your living."

Nancy's words came out in a long scream, "It is my living, and the cold, dirty streets are my home. And you're the one who drove me to them long ago. And you're the one who'll keep me there, day and night, day and night, till I die!"

She rushed at him, but Bill held her arms. She tried to get loose, and then she fainted.

Fagin wiped his forehead.

"She's all right now," said Sikes, laying her down in a corner. "She's terrible strong when she gets this way."

Charley Bates took away Oliver's new suit and locked him in a dark room. Oliver was feeling very tired and sick. He soon fell asleep.

Fagin was a wise old crook, indeed. Oliver was kept locked indoors for many days. After about a week, the Dodger and Charley Bates stayed with him from time to time. The poor boy was only too happy to see a face, no matter how bad. Charley and the Dodger told Oliver funny stories of robberies they had done. Oliver could not help but laugh. Fagin's poison was slowly working on the boy. Soon, Fagin hoped, the boy would be changed forever.

Fagin and Sikes were planning a robbery. There was a house in Chertsey with very fine silverware. Sikes was going to do the job with another robber, Toby Crackit. The plan was to have someone get in the house through a small window and then open the front door for them.

"I need a boy for the window," said Sikes. "And he must not be too big."

"Oliver is just the boy you want," said Fagin.

Sikes frowned. "What makes you take such trouble with that kid?" he asked. "There are 50 others out in the street you might pick and choose from."

"The others are no use to me, my dear," said Fagin. "The police take one look at them and know they're guilty. But this boy. . ."

Fagin knew Oliver would go with Nancy more willingly than with anyone else. So she was chosen to take Oliver to Sikes. The next night,

Nancy walked out from Fagin's, holding Oliver's hand tightly. Oliver thought about running away. As if Nancy could read his thoughts, she said, "If ever you are to get loose from here, this is not the time. I have promised that you'd be quiet. If you are not, you'll be hurt and so will I. It could even be my death. Look! This is what I got for sticking up for you." She showed him some reddish bruises on her neck and arms.

When they reached Bill Sikes's, the man loaded his gun in front of Oliver. Then he touched the cold metal to the boy's head. He said, "If you speak one word when we're out there, except when I speak to you, you better say your prayers first."

Bill Sikes and Oliver set out the next day. The boy had no idea where they were going, or what would happen. He did not dare ask. The trip was a long one, starting early in the morning. Except for a ride in a cart, they walked all the way. It was not until night that they reached the place where Toby Crackit was staying, a tumble-down house by the river. After the men had a nap, they set out, taking Oliver with them. It was half past one, foggy, and very cold.

At two o'clock they reached Chertsey. They walked to a house standing a little apart from the rest, with a wall around it. Before Oliver had time to look around, Sikes caught him under the arms. And three or four seconds later he and Toby were lying in the grass on the other side of the wall. They walked slowly toward the house.

And now, for the first time, Oliver could see the men had robbery, perhaps even murder, on their minds. He sank to his knees, full of fear and horror.

"Get up," muttered Sikes, taking his gun from his pocket. "Get up or I'll blow your brains all over the grass."

"Let me go!" said Oliver. "Let me run away, and I'll never ever come near London again!"

Sikes cocked his gun. Toby grabbed the gun and, putting his hand over Oliver's mouth, pulled him up to the house.

"Cut it out, Bill!" said Toby. "You can't shoot him here. Say another word, boy, and I'll crack you on the head. Bill, get the shutter open. The boy'll be all right."

In a minute they had the window open. Sikes whispered to Oliver, "Now listen. I'm going to put you through. Take the lantern. Go up the steps and along the hall to the street door. Open it and let us in."

Sikes pushed Oliver through the window. The boy looked back and saw Sikes pointing the gun at him. "Now!" Sikes whispered.

Oliver decided he would run up the stairs and warn the family. He started walking slowly. Then Sikes yelled suddenly, "Come back!"

Oliver's lantern fell to the floor. He saw a light and two frightened men at the top of the stairs. There was a flash followed by a loud noise and smoke. Oliver fell back to the window. Sikes grabbed him by the collar and pulled him through.

"They've hit him," said Sikes. "Quick! He's bleeding like a pig."

There was the loud ringing of a bell. Oliver felt himself being carried as Sikes ran along. Then a cold, deadly feeling came over his heart, and he saw and heard no more.

5 Old Sally's Secret

The night was terribly cold. For some people it was a night to come close to the bright fire and be thankful they were at home. For the homeless, it was a night to lie down and die.

It was this night that Mr. Bumble went to see the workhouse matron, Mrs. Corney, to talk about how difficult and ungrateful the poor were. Now, Mrs. Corney was alone, since Mr. Corney had died more than 25 years ago. But she shyly asked Mr. Bumble if he would like to stay for tea.

Mr. Bumble said yes, indeed, he would stay for tea. And he gave Mrs. Corney a look that made her face turn pink.

"Would you like it sweet, Mr. Bumble?" asked Mrs. Corney.

"Very sweet, indeed, ma'am," said Mr. Bumble, fixing his eyes on her. And if ever a beadle looked tender, Mr. Bumble did at that moment.

They sat down at a table by the fire. Mr. Bumble moved his chair closer and closer to Mrs. Corney. When he had drunk the last of his tea, Mr. Bumble wiped his lips, leaned over, and kissed her.

"Mr. Bumble!" cried Mrs. Corney in a whisper, "I shall scream!"

Mr. Bumble said nothing, but slowly put his arm around her waist.

Just then, there was a knock on the door. It was an old poor woman from the workhouse.

"If you please, mistress," said the old woman. "Old Sally is a-going, but she says she has something she must tell you before she dies."

Mrs. Corney got up with an angry face. She wondered out loud why poor people couldn't even die without bothering her. She followed the old woman outside, scolding all the way.

Left to himself, Mr. Bumble did something rather strange. He opened a drawer and counted the silverware. He looked closely at a silver milk pot to see if it was really silver. Then he put on his hat and danced four times around the table.

Meanwhile, Mrs. Corney sat at the foot of old Sally's bed. "Now listen to me," old Sally said to her. It was hard for the dying woman to get the words out. "In this very bed," Sally said, "years ago I took care of a pretty young woman. She gave birth to a boy and died. And I—I stole from her—all she had. It was gold, rich gold!"

"Gold!" said Mrs. Corney, bending eagerly over her. "Go on!"

"She trusted me, and I stole from her—and from her baby. They would have treated him better, if they had known. Oh, if someone would help that poor child!"

"The boy's name?" said Mrs. Corney.

Old Sally said, "They *called* him Oliver. The gold I stole was—"

"Yes, yes," cried Mrs. Corney. Suddenly she pulled away from the old woman. A strange noise came from old Sally's throat, and she died.

Mrs. Corney returned to her room, where Mr. Bumble was waiting. "Oh, Mr. Bumble!" she cried, "I have been so terribly put out! Those awful poor people!"

"You must take something ma'am," said Mr. Bumble. "A little wine?"

"Oh, no, I couldn't," said Mrs. Corney. "There—the top shelf in the right hand corner."

Mr. Bumble quickly filled a cup.

"Umm, I'm better now," said Mrs. Corney, after drinking half of it.

Mr. Bumble tried it, too. They sat back in their chairs, which were quite close together.

"The board gives you free coals, don't they, Mrs. Corney?" asked Mr. Bumble, squeezing her hand.

"And candles," said Mrs. Corney, giving him a shy squeeze back.

"Coals, candles, and a house rent-free," said Mr. Bumble. "Oh, Mrs. Corney, what an angel you are!"

Mrs. Corney sank into his arms.

"Did you know Mr. Slout is worse tonight, my love?" said Mr. Bumble. "He won't last a week. He is master of this workhouse. And I shall take his place! Oh, Mrs. Corney, what luck for two hearts such as ours! One little word from you, Mrs. Corney, and everything would be perfect. The one little, little word?"

"Ye—ye—yes!" sighed Mrs. Corney.

After a long and loving good-bye to his future wife, Mr. Bumble went out into the cold again. This time he went to Mr. Sowerberry's to order a coffin for old Sally.

He knocked on the door, but there was no answer. He thought perhaps Noah was in the shop, so he walked back there and looked in the window. His eyes opened wide.

Noah Claypole was sitting with his feet over the arms of an easy chair. And Charlotte was feeding him oysters.

Noah said, "I can't eat any more. Come here, Charlotte, and I'll kiss you."

"What!" cried Mr. Bumble, opening the door.

Charlotte screamed and hid her face in her apron.

"How dare you say such a thing!" said Mr. Bumble to Noah.

"It's she who's always doing it, Mr. Bumble, sir!" said Noah.

"Silence!" cried Mr. Bumble. "Kissing! Such sin and wickedness! If the government doesn't do something about this, this country will be ruined!" And with these words, Mr. Bumble left.

Fagin had been in a terrible state when Toby Crackit had come back from the robbery alone, with no idea of the fate of Oliver or Sikes. Fagin had been out all evening, trying to find out if anyone had news of Sikes. But he had had no luck at all and finally turned his steps toward home. He was about to open his door when a voice said, "Fagin! Where have you been?"

"On your business, my dear," said Fagin.

The man, whose name was Monks, came inside, and they talked in whispers. Fagin tried to calm the man, but the fellow was very angry. Monks's voice rose as he said, "I tell you, the robbery was a mistake. Why did you not get him into picking pockets, like the other boys? By this time he should have been arrested, and sent out of the country!"

Fagin said, "Oliver was not like the other boys. He was not easy to train. But now, if he's dead. . ."

"No, not that!" cried the other man. "If he's dead, it's no fault of mine! I won't have that. I told you from the first. I won't have murder; it's always found out. And it haunts a man besides. . . . What's that? The shadow of a woman?"

Fagin rushed out of the room, then walked back. "It's nothing," he said. "No one's there."

"I know I saw it!" cried Monks. His body shook. Fagin looked at him with scorn. He walked Monks all around the place, but no one was found. Finally, Monks left.

6 A Safe House

When Bill Sikes and Toby Crackit ran from the house at Chertsey, Sikes was carrying Oliver.

"Stop!" Sikes called to Toby Crackit. "Give me a hand with the boy!" He laid Oliver down in a ditch.

Toby Crackit looked back and saw that Sikes had aimed his gun at him. But Crackit could also see two men with dogs coming after them. So he ran.

Sikes looked around too. Then he left Oliver where he was and ran after Toby.

The two men chased the robbers, but it was a very cold night, and they were more than a little frightened. It wasn't long before they gave up and went back home.

Morning came, and with it came the rain. Oliver woke and cried out with pain. He rose up very weakly and tried to walk. A house was not too far off. He staggered slowly toward it. Sinking down in front of the door, he knocked.

The door was opened. A servant, Mr. Giles, looked out and said, "Why it's him!" He ran inside and called up the stairs, "It's him, Miss, it's one of the robbers! I shot him, Miss!"

"Hush!" said a soft voice. "You will frighten Mrs. Maylie. Is he hurt?"

"Very badly, Miss," said Giles. "Do you want to have a look at him?"

"Not now," said the young lady. "Bring him in, please. Poor fellow! Treat him kindly, for my sake."

Giles was gentle indeed. Dr. Losberne was sent for. While he was in an upstairs room with Oliver, two women waited.

One of the women was Mrs. Maylie. She was old and dressed in a neat, old-fashioned way. Beside her was Rose, 17 and lovely, with a thousand lights that played about her face.

Soon Dr. Losberne, a fat, good-humored gentleman, came in. "I think you had better have a look at him," said the doctor.

The women looked into the room where Oliver was sleeping. Instead of the rough-faced man they expected to see lay a child, worn with pain and exhaustion.

"This poor child cannot be a robber!" cried Mrs. Maylie.

"Wickedness has many faces," said Dr. Losberne, shaking his head.

Rose said, "But even if he has been wicked, think how young he is. He may never have known a mother's love. He may have been treated badly and forced to do wrong. Think of this, Aunt, before you let them drag the boy to prison. If not for you, I might have been as helpless as this poor child. Have pity on him before it is too late!"

"My dear love," said the old woman, taking Rose in her arms. "Do you think I would hurt a hair on his head? What can I do to save him, Doctor?"

Dr. Losberne thought for several minutes. At last he said, "If you will let me bully Giles, I think I can manage it. I don't like to do it, for he is a good servant. But you can make it up to him in a thousand ways."

The women agreed to the doctor's plan. Dr. Losberne had a long talk with Giles. At the end of it, Giles was so confused he wasn't even sure if it was Oliver that he had shot. By the time two policemen came to make a report, Giles doubted that he had shot anyone at all. So the police went away thinking Oliver had been shot in an accident and was not one of the robbers at all.

After the police left, the doctor and the two women heard Oliver's sad story from his own lips.

Oliver's sleep was peaceful and happy that night, and gentle hearts watched over him. Slowly, he grew stronger. At his request, Oliver was taken one day by Dr. Losberne to Mr. Brownlow's house. But the place was up for rent. They learned that Mr. Brownlow had gone on a trip to the West Indies. Oliver was terribly sad.

How he wished to see the old gentleman again and tell him what happened the day he disappeared!

When Oliver was well enough, the women took him with them to a cottage in the country. After a life in the crowded, dirty streets, what a joy it was for Oliver to feel the soft air, to see the green hills and rich woods!

Oliver's days at the cottage were long and peaceful. Every morning an old gentleman who lived near the church taught him lessons. Oliver learned to read better and to write. Then he would take a walk with Rose and Mrs. Maylie. The women would talk of books, or Rose would read aloud for them. In the evening, Rose would play the piano and sing. On Sundays, they would visit the clean little houses of the working people. Oliver would read a chapter or two of the Bible aloud to them.

In this way, three lovely months went by. Oliver grew closer to the kind women who had saved him, and they to him.

Summer came, and the happy days followed one after another until one beautiful night, Rose became very ill.

Mrs. Maylie sent Oliver to the village with a letter for Dr. Losberne. Oliver saw she also had a letter for her son, Harry, but she did not send it right away.

Rose quickly grew worse. The village doctor who examined her said the fever was very dangerous. "It will be a miracle if she recovers," said the young man.

When Dr. Losberne finally arrived, he stayed a long time in the sick room. When he came out, he shook his head sadly. "There is very little hope," he said.

The next morning, Oliver went out to the old churchyard. He stayed all day, crying and praying for Rose. All around him, summer burst out in all its green beauty. How could Rose die, Oliver wondered, when the world was so glad and full of life?

When Oliver came back to the cottage, he learned Rose was in a deep sleep. Either she would wake from it and recover, or she would die.

Oliver and Mrs. Maylie waited for hours, afraid to speak. At last Dr. Losberne stepped out of Rose's room.

"What news?" cried Mrs. Maylie. "Tell me at once."

The doctor said, "The danger is over. Rose will live to bless us all for years to come."

Mrs. Maylie's strength had kept her going for many long days. Now it left her, and she fell into the arms of Dr. Losberne and Oliver.

That night, Harry Maylie arrived. He was a handsome young man of about 25. After he had said hello to everyone, his mother had a talk with him alone.

"Mother," he said, "why didn't you write and send for me sooner? You know how much I care for Rose!"

"I know how much you care for her *now*," said Mrs. Maylie.

"And so will I care for her always, Mother!" said Harry.

Mrs. Maylie said, "But you are young, Harry, and have great plans for yourself. You will probably be a member of Parliament by Christmas. As for Rose, you must remember she has a stain on her name. She has never known who her parents are. If you should marry Rose, you might regret it some day. And dear Rose does not deserve such regret."

"I would be a selfish brute if I did!" said Harry.

"You think so *now*," said Mrs. Maylie.

"I will always think so," said Harry. "You think of me as a boy, Mother! I have loved Rose for years. My heart is set on her. Will you let me see her before I leave so I can tell her how I feel?"

"Of course, Harry," said his mother. "You may speak to her when she is well enough."

Some days later, when Rose was able to leave her room, Harry saw her alone. He said, "A few, a very few words I have for you, Rose. For years— years—I have loved you. I hoped to win my way to fame, and then come to tell you it had all been won for you. But here, now, with no fame won, I offer you my hand and heart."

Rose was very pale. "You have always been very kind," she said. "But there is a stain on my name. If it were not for dear Mrs. Maylie, who has raised me like I was her own child, I would be alone in this world. I have no real name, no family. I would be like a great stone; I would hold you back from rising up in the world. And now I ask you to forget me. Not as a friend, for that would hurt me deeply, but as someone to love."

Rose covered her face with one hand, and the tears fell.

After a few minutes, Harry said, "Rose, if I had no advantages of money or a good name, if I had no chance to rise to riches and honor, would you say 'yes'?"

"That can never happen," said Rose softly, "so the question is unfair, and almost unkind to ask." She gave him her hand to kiss good-bye.

But Harry caught her shoulders and pulled her to his chest. He kissed her once on her beautiful forehead and hurried from the room.

7 A Locket and a Ring

Mr. Bumble sat in the parlor of the workhouse. How different he looked! He wore a coat, but it was not *the* coat. His breeches were not *the* breeches. And instead of his mighty hat, he wore a little round one. Mr. Bumble was no longer a beadle.

He sighed loudly. "I sold myself for six teaspoons, a silver milk pot, and some secondhand furniture. I went cheap! Dirt cheap!"

Mrs. Bumble, who not long ago had been Mrs. Corney, came into the room. "Are you going to sit there all day?" she asked.

"I am going to sit here as long as I like," said Mr. Bumble. "In fact, I shall do whatever I like. That is my prerogative."

"*Your* prerogative?" said Mrs. Bumble, in a voice full of scorn.

"I said the word, ma'am," said Mr. Bumble. "The prerogative of a man is to command."

"And what's the prerogative of a woman?" asked Mrs. Bumble.

"To obey, ma'am!" said Mr. Bumble in a voice like thunder. "And I wish Mr. Corney had taught you that!"

Mrs. Bumble saw the moment had come to decide who was master in this marriage. She burst into tears, calling Mr. Bumble a hardhearted brute.

However, tears had no effect on Mr. Bumble. His heart was waterproof. He simply told her to "cry away," for it would do her good.

But if tears did not work, Mrs. Bumble had other ways. She grabbed Mr. Bumble by the throat and rained a shower of blows on him. She scratched his face and tore his hair, then pushed him over a chair.

"Get up," said Mrs. Bumble, "and take yourself away from here."

Mr. Bumble went quickly, leaving the house and walking out onto the street. The fight with his wife had made him thirsty, so he headed for a public house.

The bar was empty except for a tall stranger. After Mr. Bumble had gotten his drink, the man turned to him and said, "I think I have seen you before. You were a beadle once, weren't you?"

"I was," said Mr. Bumble, surprised.

The stranger closed the door and window and sat down next to Mr. Bumble. "Now listen to me," he said. "I came here today to look for you, and by the devil's chance you walked into the very room I was sitting in. I want an answer from you quickly—for I want to find my bed before the black night comes. The way is lonely and the night is dark, and I hate both when I am alone. Do you understand?"

"I hear you," said Mr. Bumble, "but to say I understand you would be stretching the point."

"I shall be clear enough," said the stranger. "I want some information from you. I don't ask you to give it for nothing. Do you remember a boy who was apprenticed to an undertaker? Afterwards he ran away to London."

"Why, you mean Oliver Twist!" cried Mr. Bumble. "That young rascal. . ."

"It's not him I want to know about. I've heard enough about *him*," said the stranger. "It's the old woman I want to know about. The one who took care of his mother."

Mr. Bumble told the stranger that old Sally had died. But, he said, another woman had heard a secret from her before she died.

As he listened to this news, the stranger seemed frightened. "How can I find this woman?" he asked.

"Only through me," said Mr. Bumble.

"Come tomorrow," said the stranger. "At nine o'clock." He wrote down an address on a scrap of paper. Then he got up and began to leave.

Mr. Bumble looked at the paper. "Wait," he said. "What name shall I ask for?"

"Monks," the man said and walked quickly away.

The next night, Mr. and Mrs. Bumble walked to the address Monks had given them, which was by the river Thames. It was a large building, so old that part of it had sunk down into the water.

Monks took them up a steep ladder to a room with an old table and three chairs. "Now," said Monks, as they sat down, "the sooner we get to our business, the better."

"The first question is," said Mrs. Bumble, "how much is it worth to you?"

"It may be worth 20 pounds," said Monks. "It may be worth nothing."

"Add five pounds to that 20, and I'll tell you all, not before," said Mrs. Bumble.

After some argument, Monks counted out 25 pounds in gold onto the table. "Now, begin," he said.

Mrs. Bumble said, "The old woman told me she stole from Oliver Twist's mother before she died. Then she died herself, without another word."

"That's all? That's a lie!" cried Monks in a furious voice. "I'll hear *everything* she said, or I'll tear the life out of you both!"

"The old woman didn't speak another word," said Mrs. Bumble in a calm voice. "But in her hand was a dirty scrap of paper. It was a pawn ticket, which I turned in. This is what I got for it."

She threw on the table a small leather bag. Monks grabbed it and opened it with hands that shook. Inside was a little gold locket, which held two locks of hair, and a gold wedding band.

"On the band is the name 'Agnes,' " said Mrs. Bumble. "There is a blank for the last name. And now, may I ask you a question?"

"Yes," said Monks, with some surprise.

"Can this information be used against me?" asked Mrs. Bumble.

"No," said Monks. "Look here!" He pushed the table to one side and pulled up an iron ring that was fastened to the boards of the floor. A trap door opened at Mr. Bumble's feet, making him step back quickly. Monks said, "I could have let you down quietly enough, if that had been my game." The three of them looked down below, where the black water of the river rushed by. Monks held the little bag over the water—and let it go.

"There!" said Monks, closing the trap door. "And if we meet again, there's no call for us to know each other—you understand?"

"You may count on it," said Mr. Bumble, wiping his forehead. He and Mrs. Bumble left quickly.

A few days later, Monks paid a visit to Fagin. Nancy happened to be there on an errand for

Bill Sikes. Monks frowned when he saw her. "I need to talk to you alone," he said to Fagin.

"We won't be gone but a few minutes, my dear," Fagin told Nancy. And he took Monks out of the room.

The moment they were gone, Nancy slipped off her shoes, followed them, and listened.

A quarter of an hour later, Monks had gone, and Nancy was back where the men had left her.

The next day, Bill Sikes noticed that Nancy grew excited as the evening came on. Her face was pale, and there was fire in her eyes.

"What's the matter?" he asked. "You look terrible."

"Nothing," said Nancy. "What do you look at me so hard for?

"Get me a drink," said Bill, "and come sit beside me, and put on your own face. Or I'll change it so much you won't know it."

Nancy poured out his drink, but with her back to him.

Bill said quietly to himself, "She wouldn't—no! There ain't a more loyal-hearted gal around, or I'd have cut her throat months ago."

She brought him the drink, and he drank it down. Soon he was in a deep, heavy sleep.

Nancy looked closely at his sleeping face. "The drug has taken effect," said Nancy. "But I may be too late, even now."

She ran outside and tore along the street.

"The woman is mad," said the people, turning to look after her as she ran.

In an hour, she was on a quiet, handsome street. She knocked at the door of a family inn.

"What do you want?" asked a smartly-dressed young woman.

"A lady who is staying here," said Nancy. "A Miss Maylie."

A man came to the door. He took a look at Nancy and said, "Come, none of this. Take yourself away from here."

Some of the other servants came to the door.

"I shall be carried out, if I go!" cried Nancy. "Isn't there anybody who will take a simple message from a poor woman like me?"

At this, a kind-hearted cook let her in. He took her up to a small room where she waited, her body shaking.

8 Two Spies

Rose walked lightly into the room where Nancy was waiting. "I hope no one was unkind to you downstairs," she said in her sweet voice. "I am the person you wished to see."

Rose's kind tone took Nancy by surprise. She burst into tears. "Oh, lady!" she cried. "If there were more like you in the world, there would be fewer like me—there would!"

"Sit down," said Rose. "If I can help you, I shall indeed."

"You would not treat me so kindly if you knew what I was sometimes, and that I live among thieves," said Nancy. "Is—is—that door shut?"

"Yes," said Rose. "Why?"

"Because," said Nancy, "I am about to put my life, and the lives of others, in your hands. I am the woman who dragged little Oliver back to Fagin the night he went out from Mr. Brownlow's house."

"You!" cried Rose.

"I, lady," said Nancy. "Do you know a man named Monks?"

"No," said Rose.

"He knows you," said Nancy, "and he knows you are here. That is how I found you tonight. Some time ago, I spied on him as he was talking to Fagin. Monks had seen Oliver with two of Fagin's boys the day he was taken to the police station. Monks struck a bargain with Fagin: if Fagin got the boy back, he would be paid, and if Fagin made Oliver into a thief, he would be paid even more. I saw no more of Monks until last night."

Here Nancy stopped and looked around nervously, as if Bill Sikes was somehow watching her. She went on. "Last night Monks came again, and I snuck around so I could listen. He told Fagin he had thrown all proof of Oliver's identity to the bottom of the river. He said he could take all of Oliver's money now, but he wished it had been some other way. He wished Oliver had been made a thief. But Monks swore he'd be watching Oliver for the rest of his life. He said: 'I'll lay a trap at every step my brother takes!' "

"His brother!" cried Rose.

"Yes," said Nancy. "And now I must leave, and quickly. They must never think I have come on such an errand. I must go home."

"Home!" cried Rose. "You must not go back to these people you paint in such terrible colors! If you just tell the gentleman in the next room this story, you can be taken to a place of safety in half an hour."

"Lady," said Nancy, "years ago, someone like you might have turned me from a life of sin and sadness. But it is too late!"

"It is never too late," said Rose.

"It is," cried Nancy. "I know you will not stop my going, because I have trusted in your goodness."

"But where can I find you again if I need to?" asked Rose.

"Every Sunday night, from 11 until the clock strikes 12," said Nancy, "I will walk on London Bridge, if I am alive." She moved toward the door.

"Wait another moment," said Rose. "Think about your life and the chance you have to escape it. What can hold you to it?"

Nancy said, "There is someone I cannot leave, though he may be my death. When a woman like me sets her rotten heart on a man, there is no cure. I let him fill that place which has been a blank all my life."

Nancy turned to the door. "Bless you, sweet lady. May God send as much happiness on your head as I have brought shame on mine!"

And as she sobbed out loud, Nancy left the room and ran out to the street.

Rose spent a sleepless night. She knew she must tell someone what Nancy had told her. Harry seemed the best choice, but it hurt to ask him for help. When morning came, she sat down to write him a letter. She had taken up her pen 50 times, and laid it down again, when Oliver came running into the room very excited. On a walk with Giles, he had seen Mr. Brownlow get out of a coach and enter a house. Giles had found out he lived there and had gotten the gentleman's address.

Right away, Rose sent for a coach, and she and Oliver drove to Mr. Brownlow's house. How happy Mr. Brownlow was to see Oliver again and to hear from Rose's lips how the boy was innocent of any wrong. As for Mrs. Bedwin, she had never doubted Oliver's goodness for a moment.

The same night Nancy met with Rose, a young couple came to London. It was none other than Noah Claypole and Charlotte. They came in a hurry, for they had with them 20 pounds that belonged to Mr. Sowerberry. By chance, they stopped at a public house where Fagin often went.

Noah and Charlotte sat in a back room behind the bar. On the dark wall behind their table was a pane of glass hidden by a small curtain. As Charlotte and Noah were eating, Fagin came into the bar on business.

"Hush!" said the bartender to Fagin. "Strangers in the next room."

Fagin opened the curtain a little, just as Noah was saying, "Taking 20 pounds from Mr. Sowerberry is all right, but there's plenty more to be got in this world, especially here in London. I'd like to get in with some gang of men, if only we could."

"I like that fellow's looks," whispered Fagin. He walked out from behind the bar to Noah's table. Noah was frightened indeed when Fagin told him he knew about the 20 pounds.

But Fagin said, "I only heard you by chance, my dear. You are very lucky it was only me."

In a little while, Noah was in Fagin's power and the 20 pounds were in Fagin's pocket, as payment for joining the gang.

A few days later, Fagin had a job for Noah. Nancy had been acting strange lately. Fagin guessed she had grown tired of Bill Sikes and had found someone new. Perhaps, thought Fagin, Nancy could be talked into poisoning Sikes. Then she would be free of him, and Fagin

would be free as well. And, knowing of her crime, Fagin would have more power over her than ever.

"I want you to follow her," said Fagin to Noah. "See where she goes, and who she meets, and report all you see to me alone."

9 Murder!

The clocks chimed three-quarters past 11 as two people walked out on London Bridge. The first was Nancy, who looked about her with frightened eyes. The second, walking a good way behind her in the deep shadows, was Noah Claypole. Nancy waited at the center of the bridge.

At two minutes after 12, a coach pulled up at one end of the bridge. Rose Maylie and Mr. Brownlow got out. Nancy hurried up to them. "Not here," she said. "I am afraid to speak to you here! Come away from the road and down the steps over there."

They followed her down the dark steps, where they would be hidden from sight. When he saw where they were headed, Noah slipped close to them and hid around a corner.

Mr. Brownlow said, "You have placed your trust in us, and now I shall place my trust in you. Here is what we have planned: to capture Monks and make him confess the secret of Oliver's birth. If we cannot get Monks, you must help us capture Fagin."

"I cannot!" cried Nancy. "I will never do it!"

"Tell me why," said Mr. Brownlow.

"For one reason," said Nancy. "Bad as Fagin is, and bad as he's treated me, I've led a horrible life, too. I won't turn on them—any of them—just as they haven't turned on me."

"Then help me find Monks," said Mr. Brownlow. "If he turns on the others, we shall not go after them. They shall go free."

"I have been among liars since I was a child," said Nancy, after a silence. "But I will take your word."

In such a low voice that Noah could hardly hear, she told them where Monks could be found. She then said, "He is tall and strong-looking. His face is dark; his eyes are sunken. When he walks, he always looks over his shoulder. And on his throat there is. . ."

"A wide red mark, like a burn?" cried Mr. Brownlow.

"How's this?" cried Nancy. "You know him!"

"I think I do," said Mr. Brownlow. "We shall see. And now that you have helped us, we offer our help to you. We cannot give you peace of mind, but we can give you a safe place here in England. Or, if you wish, in another country."

"I cannot, sir," said Nancy. "I hate my life now, but I—I am chained to it. I must go. I must go

home. A fear has been with me all day, a fear that burns me like fire. I have horrible thoughts of death. I must go now!"

Nancy left, crying bitter tears. Mr. Brownlow sadly led Rose away. As soon as everyone had gone, Noah Claypole ran for Fagin's house as fast as his legs could carry him.

An hour later, Fagin knew everything. He was half mad with fury. He did not believe Nancy had refused to turn him in. He sent for Bill Sikes and told him what Nancy had done.

Sikes said nothing. The story over, he rushed to the door. "Wait!" cried Fagin. "You won't be too—violent, Bill?"

It was almost daylight, light enough for each man to see the face of the other. There was a fire in the eyes of both, which could not be mistaken.

"I mean," said Fagin, "not too violent for safety. Be careful, Bill."

Bill said not a word and rushed out into the silent streets. He did not stop until he reached his room.

Nancy was on the bed asleep. "Get up," Bill said.

She looked up and saw the light of day. She moved to open the curtain.

He pulled her hand away. "Let it be," he said. "It's light enough for what I've got to do."

"Bill," said Nancy in a frightened voice. "Why do you look like that at me!"

He grabbed her by her head and throat and dragged her to the center of the room.

"Bill, Bill," cried Nancy as she pulled away with the strength of her fear. "Tell me what I've done!"

"You know, you she-devil!" cried Bill. "You were watched tonight! Every word you said was heard!"

"Then spare my life, as I spared yours!" she cried. "Think of all I gave up tonight for you! I have been true to you. On my guilty soul I have!" She grabbed hold of him. He could not tear her away.

She said, "Let me see those people again. I will beg them to show you the kindness they showed me. Then we'll leave this awful place. Far apart we'll find better lives, and forget how we used to live. It's never too late! They told me so! I feel it now. But we must have time—a little, little time!"

Bill pulled one arm free and grabbed his gun. Somehow in his fury, he remembered he must be careful. He hit her with it twice with all his strength.

She fell on her knees and raised her hands toward heaven. It was a terrible thing to see. Bill staggered back and, shutting out the sight with his hand, grabbed a heavy club and struck her down.

The bright sun poured in the window. It lit up the room where the murdered woman lay. He tried to shut it out, but it would pour in. At last he got up, locked the room, and left.

He walked out of the city, then back again, with his dog following close behind. He walked up and down fields, rested in ditches, then walked over the same fields again.

He walked to Hendon. That was a good place, he thought, not too far off. But when he got there, everyone seemed to look at him strangely. Morning and noon passed, and the day was getting dark. Still he walked.

At last, very tired and hungry, he stopped at a public house. He was sitting, almost asleep, when a man came in selling all sorts of things. He had razors, medicine, cosmetics, cheap perfume. Men sat around him, looking at all he had to sell.

"What's that?" asked one man, pointing to a small, hard cake of stuff.

"This," said the fellow, "will get rid of any sort of stain. Wine stains, fruit stains, beer stains, water stains. . . . If a lady stains her honor, she only has to eat one of these, for it's poison! One penny each! Why, I'll show you how beautiful it works! I'll get the stain out of this gentleman's hat before he can buy me a pint of beer!"

"Give that back!" cried Sikes, starting up.

"I'll clean it out, sir," said the man, whether it's a wine stain, paint stain, bloodstain. . . ."

The man got no further. Sikes pushed over the table, tore the hat from him, and rushed out of the house.

He walked. Nancy's body seemed to follow his every step. He walked until he could not take another step, and he lay down next to a wall. But then a new horror came. It was her eyes, so empty of light. They were everywhere.

When morning came, he decided to risk going back to London. He could hide out. He'd force Fagin to give him money. Then he could leave for another country. The dog, though. The dog would give him away. He walked until he came to a pond. Then he picked up a heavy stone and tied it in his handkerchief.

"Come here," he called to the dog.

But as he tried to tie the handkerchief to the dog's throat, the animal growled and moved away.

"Come back here!" called Sikes.

Slowly the dog came forward a little. Then he stopped, turned, and ran away as quickly as he could.

Sikes waited awhile, but the dog did not come back. At last, he began walking toward London alone.

10 Secrets Come to Light

It was late evening when a coach pulled up to Mr. Brownlow's door. Mr. Brownlow got out, along with two strong-looking men. The men led a third fellow up to the door. This man was Monks.

"What right have you to kidnap me on the street and bring me here?" said Monks to Mr. Brownlow.

"Be quiet," said Mr. Brownlow. "And if you try to leave, I shall have you arrested for fraud and robbery."

Mr. Brownlow's men brought Monks inside.

"This is fine treatment from my father's oldest friend," said Monks.

"It is *because* I was your father's oldest friend," said Mr. Brownlow.

After a long silence, Monks spoke. "What do you want with me?" he said.

"I shall tell you what I know," said Mr. Brownlow, "and then you shall see what I want. When your father was but a boy he was forced into marriage with a woman ten years older than he. After years of unhappiness, the couple went their separate ways. They had one child, and that child was *you*, Edward Leeford."

Monks sat with the face of a man who would deny everything.

"As you know," Mr. Brownlow went on, "about the time your father was 30 and you were 11, your father met new friends. He met a retired army officer who had two daughters. The younger daughter was only two or three years old. The older was a beautiful girl of 19. She fell deeply in love with your father, and he with her. In a year, they were pledged to each other."

"I know nothing of all this," said Monks, biting his lip.

Mr. Brownlow said, "Your manner tells me you have never forgotten it, and never stopped thinking of it with a bitter heart.

"An uncle of your father's died in Rome," Mr. Brownlow continued. "Your father had to go there immediately, for the uncle had left him money. Before he set out on the trip, he came to London. He left some things with me. One was a portrait of the girl he loved. That was the last time I saw him. Soon after your father arrived in Rome, he died. I went in search of the girl. I wanted to offer her comfort for her loss and the shame of a guilty love. But she and her family had disappeared."

Monks began to breathe easier and smile.

"But by chance, your younger brother Oliver was cast my way," said Mr. Brownlow.

"What?" said Monks.

"I was able to save him from a life of wrong," said Mr. Brownlow, "and while he was with me, I was struck by his strong likeness to the girl in the portrait. Then the boy was lost to me. Since your mother was dead, I knew that only you could solve the mystery. The last I had heard, you were in the West Indies. I went there in search of you, only to find you had returned to London. I had no luck in finding you, until two hours ago."

"And now what have you against me?" said Monks, boldly. "That some young boy looked like some girl's portrait? You don't even know if my father had another child! You don't even know that."

"I *did* not," said Mr. Brownlow, "but in the last two weeks I have learned everything. There was a will, which your mother destroyed. It mentioned a child which was born to the girl and your father. There was proof of his birth and of his parents. It was destroyed by you. As you told Fagin, *All proof of Oliver's identity lies at the bottom of the river.*"

"No!" cried Monks, overwhelmed by these charges.

"Every word that has passed between you and Fagin is known to me," said Mr. Brownlow. "Shadows on the wall have caught your whispers. A woman who had pity for a child was brave, indeed. Now murder has been done, and you are partly to blame."

"No, no," said Monks. "I thought Nancy and Sikes had an argument."

"She died because she told some of your secrets," said Mr. Brownlow. "Will you tell all of them, now? Will you write a statement of truth before witnesses?"

"Yes," said Monks in a low voice. "I will."

"You must do more than that," said Mr. Brownlow. "You have not forgotten what the will promised for Oliver. You must give him what he is owed."

Monks walked up and down, wondering how he could get out of giving Oliver his share of their father's money. All at once the door was quickly unlocked. Dr. Losberne rushed in and said, "Bill Sikes will be taken—tonight! His dog has been seen at an old house where Sikes used to go. There is no doubt that Sikes himself will show up soon."

"What of Fagin?" asked Mr. Brownlow.

"He is sure to be captured soon," said Dr. Losberne.

Mr. Brownlow turned to Monks. "Have you made up your mind?" he said.

"Yes," said Monks. "You—you will not turn me in?"

"I will not," said Mr. Brownlow. "Stay here. It is your only hope of safety."

The two men locked the door and left in a fever of excitement.

11 A Monster Dies

On the south side of the river Thames is Jacob's Island. It was once a busy place. Now the buildings are slowly falling down into the mud. Garbage and rot are everywhere. No one goes there unless they are terribly poor—or have no other place to hide.

In one of these buildings, hid Toby Crackit and another of Fagin's men, Tom Chitling. They sat nervously, thinking about what had just happened and wondering what would happen next.

"When was Fagin caught?" asked Toby Crackit.

"Just before dinner," said Tom. "Charley Bates and I made it up the chimney. Charley should be here soon. But Noah was caught, along with Fagin." He went on, "It was awful when they took Fagin away." He bit his lip. "The crowd was all around him, snarling and trying to get at him. The police fought them like devils. Fagin was muddy and bleeding and holding on to the police like they were his dearest friends. I can still hear the cries of the women. They said they'd tear his heart out!"

Tom got up and walked around the room. A minute later, they heard a noise from the open window below. Then Sikes's dog came up the stairs and into the room.

"What's this?" said Toby. "I—I hope *he* isn't coming here."

Tom agreed. Several hours passed, and Sikes did not appear. They decided he must have gone out of the country and left the dog behind.

Night fell and there was a knock downstairs.

"That'll be Charley Bates," said Toby. He hurried down the stairs.

It was Bill Sikes. His face was white, his breath was short and thick. It was the very ghost of the man.

A minute later, there was another knock. Toby went downstairs and came back with Charley Bates. When Charley saw Bill Sikes, he fell back. "Why didn't you tell me *he* was here?" Charley asked.

"Charley," said Sikes, "Don't you—don't you know me? I'm your friend."

There was horror in the boy's face. "Don't come near me," he said, "you monster!"

Sikes's eyes sunk to the ground.

"I'm not afraid of you!" cried Charley, shaking his fist. "If they come after you, I'll give you up! You may kill me for it, if you like, or if you dare.

But if I can, I'll give you up. Murderer! Help! Murderer! Help!"

With these cries, the boy threw himself on Bill Sikes. The big man was so surprised, he fell to the ground.

The boy and the man rolled on the ground. Toby and Tom stared at them, unable to move. Charley held on to Sikes, calling for help with all his strength. Soon Sikes had him down, with his knee on his throat. But Toby Crackit pulled Sikes off the boy and pointed to the window.

Lights gleamed below. There were voices and the sound of many footsteps hurrying across the nearest wooden bridge.

"Help!" screamed Charley in a voice that tore the air. "He's in here!"

Sikes grabbed the boy. "Where can I lock him up? That door!" He threw the boy in and turned the key.

"Is the door downstairs locked and chained?" Sikes asked.

"Locked, chained, and lined with sheet iron. The windows, too," said Tom.

Sikes called out the window to the crowd. "Do your worst! I'll fool you yet!"

The angry crowd answered with a terrible roar. The people waved back and forth in the darkness below like a field of corn driven by an angry wind. A man on a horse shouted, "I'll give 20 pounds to the man who brings me a ladder!"

Others took up the cry.

Sikes decided to go up on the roof. There was one chance to escape, he thought. If he could drop down into the muddy ditch next to the house he might lose himself in the dark moving crowd.

"Give me a rope," he said to Tom and Toby, "or I shall do two more murders and kill myself."

A strong rope was quickly found. Sikes hurried up to the roof.

The crowd grew. People climbed to the tops of the houses around him. The small bridges of the island bent under the people's weight. The night rang with their angry shouts and screams.

Sikes tied one end of the rope to the chimney. The other end he made into a noose and brought the loop over his head. He was about to bring it down around his waist when suddenly he looked around and screamed, "Her eyes!"

He staggered as if struck by lightning and fell over the edge of the roof. The noose was still around his neck. His weight pulled it tight, and he shot down like an arrow. He fell 35 feet. The rope jerked tight around his neck, and there he hung.

Two days after Bill Sikes's death, two coaches drove to the town where Oliver was born. In one were Oliver, Rose, Mrs. Maylie, Mrs. Bedwin, and Dr. Losberne. In the other were Mr. Brownlow and Monks.

They stayed in a fine hotel, which Oliver used to stare at in wonder when he was a poor workhouse boy. And in that hotel, Oliver learned all the secrets of his birth. It was a shock to meet Monks, and to learn he was the boy's own brother. Mr. Brownlow drew Oliver close to his side and said to Monks, "This is your half brother, the illegitimate son of your father, my dear friend Leeford, by poor Agnes Fleming, who died after giving birth to him." Monks turned away, a look of hate on his face.

While Oliver listened, Monks confessed to Mr. Brownlow that his mother had taken two letters from his father. The letters were written by Leeford himself before he died, addressed to Mr. Brownlow. One was to be given to Agnes Fleming. In it, Leeford confessed he had made up some story, some mystery, why he could not marry her right away. She had gone on, patiently trusting him, until she lost what no one could ever give her back. He reminded her of the day he had given her the locket and the ring, and said how he hoped to engrave his name on the ring some day.

The second letter was Leeford's will. It left little money to his wife and Monks, for both had given him much pain. The wife hated him deeply, and the boy, a wild, wicked child, had been taught to hate him from birth. Most of the money was left to Agnes and the child she might have. If the child was a girl, the money would be given freely. But a boy must prove himself. If he came to wrong, he would receive no money.

Monks confessed that he had paid Fagin to lead Oliver into a life of crime. He also admitted that his mother burned the will and kept the letter. And he himself destroyed the ring and locket that the Bumbles gave him.

Then Mr. Brownlow brought in Mr. and Mrs. Bumble. They had no choice but to confess as well. Mr. Brownlow said he would make sure they both lost their jobs as punishment for what they had done.

"It was all Mrs. Bumble," said Mr. Bumble, first making sure his wife had left the room. "She *wanted* to do it."

"That is no excuse," said Mr. Brownlow. "You were there when the ring and locket were destroyed. In the eye of the law, you are more guilty, for the law supposes that your wife acts as you tell her to."

"If the law supposes that," said Mr. Bumble, "then the law is an idiot!" And he followed his wife out of the room.

Oliver's tears had fallen fast as he heard the secrets of his mother and father. But his tears changed to joy when one last secret came to light: Agnes had a younger sister, and this sister was Rose. Rose was Oliver's aunt!

Oliver threw his arms around her. "I'll never call you aunt," he cried. "Sister! My own dear sister! Someone that my heart loved so dearly from the first!"

The orphan children had found each other. The others left them alone for a while. Then came a soft knock at the door. Oliver left, and Harry Maylie came in.

"I have given up all dreams of riches and glory," Harry said to Rose. "Now England's rich countryside and a village church—my own—would make me prouder than all the hopes I had before. This is the life I offer you, and my heart as well."

Soon Oliver and the others were giving their good wishes to the joyful bride- and groom-to-be.

12 The End of Many Stories

The courtroom was filled, from floor to roof, with human faces. And all eyes were on Fagin.

He stood there, watching and listening to the judge. Only his eyes moved.

The jury left the room. A jailer led him to a chair. He followed as if asleep.

A long wait—and at last the jury returned. There was perfect silence in the court. Then the word: guilty.

The courtroom rang with a great shout, and another, and another. And the crowd outside shouted joyfully with the news that Fagin would die on Monday.

He was taken to a cell and left alone. He sat on a stone bench opposite the door and remembered the judge's words. He thought of men he had seen die. They had been hanged— live men turned into dangling heaps of clothes!

The day passed off. Day? There was no day; it was gone as soon as it had come. Night came on again; night so long in its awful silence, yet so short with its fleeting hours.

The day broke. Sunday. One more day to live. He was awake, yet dreaming. His dirty skin

seemed to burn with a fever of anger and fear. His breath came short. He hurried back and forth in his cell. The jailers kept watch on him now, but they could not watch alone, for Fagin was too awful to see. Two men kept watch together.

Monday morning came. A great crowd was already gathered at the prison. The people played cards, laughed, and joked. Everything seemed full of life. But there, in the middle of the crowd, was the black stage of the scaffold and the hanging rope—the terrible workings of death.

There is little more to tell of this story. What became of the characters shall be told in a few simple words.

Before three months had passed, Rose and Harry were married. Harry became the pastor of the village church. Mrs. Maylie lived out the rest of her days with her son and his wife. Rose grew into sweet and lovely womanhood. In the years that followed, her own happy children were always at her knee, and a thousand looks and smiles were shared between them.

Soon after the marriage, Dr. Losberne became very unhappy with London. At last he moved to the country, near the village and church of his young friend Harry. He became an expert at gardening, fishing, and carpentry. Mr. Grimwig became a close friend of his, and visits him often.

Oliver gave some of the money from his father to Monks. But Monks fell into his old ways, spent it all, and died in prison.

In return for telling the police all he knew about Fagin, Noah Claypole was set free. He and Charlotte now make a living without working too hard. What they do is take a walk on a Sunday, in their best clothes. When they are in front of a public house, Charlotte pretends to faint. The kind owner brings a bit of brandy for poor Charlotte. The next day, Noah tells the police the public house has broken the law and served liquor on a Sunday, and he is paid for his information.

Mr. and Mrs. Bumble, after losing their jobs, became extremely poor and ended up in the very workhouse where Oliver began his life. Mr. Bumble's spirits have sunk so low he is not even happy to be separated from his wife.

Master Charley Bates turned his back on a life of crime. After some very hard times, he found work with a farmer and now is the happiest herdsman in all Northamptonshire.

Mr. Brownlow adopted Oliver and moved with him and Mrs. Bedwin to the country, less than a mile away from Harry Maylie's church. With his dear friends close by, Oliver got the last wish of his warm and earnest heart. And the little group of people living near the church enjoy almost perfect happiness in this ever-changing world.

In the altar of Harry Maylie's church is a white stone tablet with the name "Agnes" written upon it. It is believed that the spirit of Agnes Fleming sometimes comes to that altar—even though the spot is in a church, and even though she was weak and died in shame.